The
Poetic
Thoughts
and
Verses
of
Louie
Bellson

Compiled and Edited by
Dave Black

Cover art by Louie Bellson

T0057219

HUDSON MUSIC.

Table of Contents

INTRODUCTION

I remember talking to Louie at his home one day and asking if he had any hobbies outside of music. I was surprised to hear that he loved to write poetry and do pencil drawings. When I asked if he had anything I could read, he pulled out two small pamphlets he had put together called *The Poetic Thoughts and Verses of Louie Bellson, 1* and *2*. Those two pamphlets were bound with staples and wrapped with a simple cover made from construction paper.

After reading the two small books, which contained over 100 thoughts and verses, I was impressed with what he had written and suggested we do a more professional-looking edition that combined the best of both books. The first updated publication, which I also selected and edited, came out in 1986 and was primarily given as a gift to family and friends for various occasions.

It has always been my hope that this small book of poetry would be made available to a wider audience, and so I'm thankful to both Rob Wallis and Hudson Music not only for their love and support of Louie, but for their willingness to make this new edition available to the general public.

Dave Black
Los Angeles, CA, 2020

FOREWORD

I think I have always had a flair for poetry because to me, poetry is like writing lyrics for music. They are both full of expression, feeling, and emotion. I like to put my thoughts and expressions into words, for they are soulful and a part of my life.

The writings contained in this book are based on my actual experiences and views of life. I would love to paint and sketch someday. My poems in this book are my paintings in words.

June Bellon

"WHY CAN'T WE?"

"IF THE SUN CAN WARM THE AIR
AND BIRDS FLY ANYWHERE –
WHY CAN'T WE?"

"IF THE MOON CAN KISS THE STARS
AND DREAMS CAN REACH TO MARS –
WHY CAN'T WE?"

I KNOW YOUR WAY IS FREE –
THE FUTURE IS TO BE –
I'M LIKE A PLAYFUL TOY –
BOUNCING TO YOU WITH JOY –

"IF THE MOUNTAINS TOUCH THE SKY
AND FEEL THE MAGIC HIGH –
WHY CAN'T WE?
YES!
WHY CAN'T WE?"

By Louie Bellson
10/19/91

Written in 1991 during the National Drum Association Convention in Chicago, while reflecting on both the young drummers and their dreams, and his recently departed wife, Pearl.

The Power of Time

While we were young, the energies flowed through the excitement of the elderly.

The air was pure; anticipation reigned throughout each day. As the body stretched into the form of a huge ball rolling into oblivion, the task of survival became the prime goal.

The hunter sharpened his tools, and the hunted kept running for peace.

What was wrong? What was right?

Suddenly the sky took on a grey hue and the wind gave a warning of danger.

Face up to it or fall.

You know how to smile because you have cried.

You know how to speak because you've been silent.

I don't need the power of stress to test me—

I can get along without anyone.

Leave me be.

As the tones in my head come to an easier tempo, my silent discussion has me in a fixation.

Trapped as you are, you know there is a secret passageway out.

Keep looking. Keep trying. It's there, and when you find it, you'll hold onto it like a sacred jewel.

You will speak of it with love and transfer its meaning to those you love.

Columbia River

During the day she glimmers like a proud diamond in the sun. Her beautiful surroundings afford her a garment that is irresistible. At night she is a huge black pearl brooding her lament to the sky. Forever she is breathtaking, and forever she will be known as one of God's miracles.

The Rhythm of the Train

A - click - a - clack - a - whack
Go the wheels against the track.
The hands, feet, and mind
Join the syncopated find.
Whatever else is stirring,
The over-taxing soul.
This moment of purring
Seems to be the right goal.

Christmas

Christmas! Christmas! and what it brings,
Such wonderful gifts and other things,
By other things I really mean
Heartfelt sincerity that is not seen;
Let's spread the friendship and good cheer,
And have a Merry Christmas
And a Happy New Year.

A Silent Thought to a Man

(Written November 24, 1963 on a train from Chicago, Illinois to Los Angeles, California.)

Dear Beloved President:

Today, all over the world, the bells toll. Today, all over the world, people pray for your soul. We ask why this terrible tragedy has come to pass. We do not question the scrutiny of our Lord and we know destiny rewinds. We stumble in shame and sadness as we realize your sacrifice was for our ignorance and troubled awakening. Was it meant for a sudden change in our attitudes toward one another, which are now only hate and resentment? Yes, we bow our heads and ask for more help as we have in the past. History is to teach us. As yet, we haven't learned, we haven't loved; it has almost been a total waste. Dear Beloved President, I pray to Almighty God that your sacrifice has finally given the world the sense to join together in work and the love to make a strong, free, and honest world. You have gone to your resting place. As we who live, must die, our meeting is inevitable. When we meet, I hope all our messages will be, Dear President: Your work was not in vain; your energy, everlasting loyalty, love, and sacrifice have meant a new life to the world.

My Prayer

My prayer is for the children. They entered the world with no hate, clear minds, warm hearts, and the ability to make friends with everyone. For those youngsters, the unfortunate, the crippled, the afflicted in some way, I pray they find the road to mend their health, that they may have the privilege of every human: the right to good health, happiness, and love. Our only salvation is the youth of today. If they are not taught the value of true friendship and love, we are indeed a perilous earth with time escorting us into complete oblivion. My prayer is also for the grown people: for those who have material wealth and think life is based on the ownership of dollars. May they enjoy their good fortune, but make them realize that the health and companionship of our loved ones can never be bought with all the dollars in the world. For those who discriminate, make them realize that God placed everyone on earth to be treated equal and to be loved by one another. Make them realize that they cannot change the plan of our Lord. We are having turmoil and wars today because humans are rebelling against the basic rules of God. They are becoming mass murderers and losing their conception of love. Make them realize their fate before it is too late. Let's pray for our health and pray that God will lead us to work, love and guide one another in making this a beautiful world.

Today (a Flower Fell)

Today the skies cry. They spill their tears on a land that is parched and dry from the lack of love. The cracks in the earth have swallowed the beautiful flowers and destroyed the roots of all the colors. Today, a special flower fell and died—one that had an extra-strong root. It had all the colors and was strong with love and understanding. Maybe the tears will water new roots and allow new flowers of all colors to bloom and grow in the warmth of sunshine, stand tall with love, and forever expel a fragrance of freshness and happiness. Oh, yes! I see it, I feel it, I know it will happen.

~~~~~~~~~~

Flying High Above the Clouds

As I gaze at the horizon, which is many times inflated, I ask myself, "Is it possible without drink, to be so intoxicated?"

Pink, rose, then a sudden burst of red. The sea of clouds form the white waters that introduce a horizon so magnificent in color.

The shape changes. First a city, then a river, then a giant dog.

The thoughts are many, the questions unanswered. We are sure of one thing, however:

This is an unforgettable creation that no living person can equal.

A Man and His Drums

I quietly, with Peace and Love, roar like the thunder
in the sky and sound the heartbeat of life.

Blue

(Written to Blue Mitchell's wife, Thelma)

Dear, Dear Thelma:

I too mourn the loss of our friend.
Our blessings are to be counted because we were
able to share many happy moments with Blue.
Can you imagine if we didn't have any?
Blue's tempo was chosen.
His clear, true, round, and beautiful sound paved
the way.
If our key matches, we will reach his horizon and
measure life's song to the end.

Javile

A little learnin' is like a love-in:
You can never get enough.

Harold Arlen's Music

Somewhere Over the Rainbow all of us come to realize that *Stormy Weather* and *Ill Wind* are not forever. We reach a point during our lives of uncertainty wondering if *Happiness Is a Thing Called Joe* or *It's Only a Paper Moon* for sure. Yes, this is depressing, but don't forget, That *Old Black Magic* seems to always come through, and when it does, you say to yourself, *What's Good About Goodbye? Let's Fall in Love*. We need no sorrow, no regrets, no *Blues in the Night*, because when we grow old, we want to remember *Last Night* when *We Were Young*. So we conquer something, a feeling—and what a feeling! We keep repeating, *Come Rain or Come Shine*; what a happy soul I am, for *I've Got the World on a String*.

As Long as...

As long as we can love, we can live.
As long as we can be together, we can survive.
To live and survive *peacefully* is the best concert any two people have.

Play the Role

Play the role of a scholar—
Play the role of a doctor—
Play the role of a bum—
But never play anyone CHEAP.

~~~~~~~~~~~~~~~~~~~~~~~~~~~~~~

Tempo Di Learn-O

You can have the big, big towns
Where all the girls wear silken gowns
And the pace is too fast.
Give me the country life
Where I know it's a good life
And I can lose the good old past.
You can run from day to night
And hope you won't get in a fight
Because the tension is too high.
I'll take the easy time
Sing a tune that really rhythms
I know that this will get me by.
Why fight the crowd
And listen to music that's too loud?
Take the natural way
With Peace and Love each precious day.
You can have the early calls
And dread the long and boring balls
And know you have to do it all your life.
I'll wake up at my time
Break some bread with friends of mine
And know this is my kind of life.

Changes

The green leaves of summer fade to the colors of a painter's much-used palette.

Then in winter, they tumble to the ground, cradle their creator's roots, and care for his being till spring and the birth of his new family.

The green Earth gives way to a huge white blanket, and the air bites at those who challenge it. The beauty is the same, but there are changes.

Changes in the sky, changes in the days, changes in the sun and moon, and changes in the stars that sometimes glitter bright.

But you never change. Your summer air is as concerning in the winter. Your strength always bends to the task. However somber, you sing to the end, but you never change. Why? Because when you rest your head on my shoulder, I know what you are and love is forever— *it doesn't change.*

What Matters

Color us red, for the inner core flows of this substance. The rest really doesn't matter, does it? We walk and talk —breathe and die as one. You only differ in your name. Your letters are different than mine.

Survival

When you've completed the task,
They will ask,
What took you so long?

If the job is undone,
They know they have won,
The right to say you are wrong.

When you've given your all,
Are about to fall,
No one will catch you,
But God will protect you.

The loneliness is your hour,
God is your power.
Only you need to know
That God's light will make you grow.

~~~~~~~~~~~~~~~~~

Sudden Inspiration

Here I wait in silent bliss,
To hold your hand and then to kiss.
Now I pray for you to stay,
So fresh and pure till our ending day.

Will You Take Me Away?

Will you take me away from the canyons of steel
And make me feel real again?

Will you take me to where the fields are so green
And they can be seen for miles?

Let the sweetness of the air cleanse my body of despair.
Let me hear the pure sounds from nature's calling
grounds,
Country Me, Country Me, Country Me.

Will you take me away from the turbulent skies
And make these eyes see the rain?

Will you take me to places where I can see
Faces of people with smiles?

Let me touch the earth and my body give birth
To a feeling of joy only one can enjoy,
Country Me, Country Me, Country Me.

Watch me, touch me, hold me, think me,
Hear me, free me, sweet me, and love me.

Will you take me away from the long lonely night
And ease me from fright and pain?

Will you take me to where the night won't be long
And I will belong to our styles?

Let me toil the lands with these strong hands
And grow the things even loved by kings,
Country Me, Country Me, Country Me.

Fairyland

In heated despair and crumbling nervousness,
The craving to vanish suddenly comes to mind.
The aesthetic portion of my acumen rises
And then guides me to a place where naturals of beauty
are the ways of life.
There I find the sweet-smelling air washing the pretty
green trees.
And playing with the gaily-colored flowers.
A sea of blue, glistening with beauty,
A sound now and then of its white tinkling toes splashing
against the sandy shore.
A song of happiness can be heard, and it tingles through
and through.
Right then, the feeling is strange
For to have missed all this fairyland brings back the
thought of another world.
Cruel, emaciated, neurotic, to-be-pitied Souls plunged to
the depths of hatred.
This is our conception of life
So let us all find ourselves
And live for the grace and love we were meant for.
Come, let us find this fairyland
And Live! Live! Live!

The Sun, Moon, and Stars Through Tears

Today I stop to realize my recovery of yesterday and hope my wounds from tomorrow won't be too severe. As the sun rises, my eyes are blurred by the rays of the big red ball of warmth. The tears from my eyes are hopeful signs of Peace and Love, but as the day wears on and I look at the moon and stars through blurred eyes, I know these tears cry out for the lonely, sick, and tormented people all over the world.

~~~~~~~~~~~~

A Form of Blues

I'm blue because you're away,
But my color will come back someday.
When I see you, I'll have a different hue.
It will match the color of your words.

~~~~~~~~~~~~

Unfortunate Circumstance

We are giants of sin and destruction, but mere infants of love and construction.

A Day of Her Being

As the orange glow starts to paint the sky and warm the cool air, the muscles in her hands start to guide the sights of a new day.

As the morning sounds envelope the city, her head orchestrates the motions of her body.

A deep sigh, a silent prayer, and open eyes to face the world.

The sky becomes a huge ball of fire on a blue lawn. The energy reaches her body, and the hands beckon to the needy.

The morning humors the masses, and she's already proven her worth. The afternoon hustle has given proof of her honesty.

When the evening quiets the tension, her chores have stunned the light to a dark, honest hue.

The giant gives thanks for her being. Another day has peaked its ritual dance, and she's made it into a prayer of love for everyone.

United We Stand—Divided We Fall

The voices spark the early morning air, but the darkness still has the edge of day. Sweet words, harsh words, vamp 'til noon, but the gray skies still cry silently. Busy feet, hands full of papers, command the afternoon, but the street scene struggles to survive. The day ends with laughter and sadness; will the voices be heard? Will the moon make us smile?

Let your words of wisdom touch the skin of my body, and let me feel that we are one, or the future will separate us forever, and our worlds will be strange and unfriendly. Come to my world and lift me to yours; I will listen if you talk with me.

Abidjan,
Ivory Coast
Africa
7/2/76

~~~~~~~~~~~~~~~~

Talkin' to Myself

Put in a good word for me.

Acceptance

If you tune to my strings,
We will make melodies of love.
If you sing with me sweetly,
Our voices will echo above.
If you hold out your hand
With a twinkle in your eye,
You'll make roses grow in winter
And snowflakes fall in July.

Try the mountains for your high.
Take in the fragrance of the flowers.
Stand in wonder of the silence
And care not of tomorrows.

If we let nature sing it's song
And we join to its refrain,
The snows will water the roses
And then we can't complain.

That Face

That face—just look at that face!
It is a masterpiece that only God gave;
It knows no malice, no hardship, no confusion;
Eyes so soft and lovingly true,
This face says happiness and smiles forever.

What a pretty face!
With all that lovely grace;
If this isn't love, I'm through.
When your eyes meet mine,
I know that it's my time.
If this isn't love, I'm through.
If you tell me once, that you'll love me always,
I will sing and shout all the rest of our days.
Come with me and see
Just what our plans will be.
I'm sure you won't regret it
And know you won't forget it.
If this isn't love, I'm through!

Mr. Riley

Our gallant little champ who is constantly on the vamp.
Exploring his glittering face and showing off his elegant
grace. He strides like the ponies—flashing his gestures
supreme. Adding gaiety to the old cronies, and definitely
a child's dream. This, human, is a mark of love, health,
and happiness—it's our Mr. Riley (a dog).

Our World Today

Oh, Lord, please grant these fighting men a pardon for
all their brutal sin. They know not fear and have the taste
to kill or hate one another and destroy at will. They fight
for a cause with death as applause. They wash the earth
with red, rich blood and die in vain, no reward but mud.
No remembrance, no cries, no thanks, no sights. They
are forgotten and lost even though they've paid a heavy
cost. Why must they strive for everyone's life when we
all could be so happy and free? Lord, help these sick
and troubled nations to sign their much-needed
resignations. Make them understand the value of lives
lived instead of the guns and cannons and knives. God,
bless these men, and keep them to win an everlasting
peace they tried to increase. Guide us to a world of
friendly thoughtfulness, and teach us the importance of
love and complete happiness.

Friends

With you as my friend
I will always mature
With strength and dedicate myself
To the teachings you have bestowed upon me.

My flower will stay in bloom
Because of your warm sunshine
And soft raindrops of love.

Together, our instrument of peace
Will overcome any discord and produce
Tones of happiness.

Just Wondering

First, there were birds of a natural feather,
Now there are giants controlling the weather.
Huge monsters of metal soaring thru space.
To compete with time at a tremendous pace.
An unbelievable sight
By day or night.
To see these huge birds
Is a description beyond words.
As we watch them racing to the skies,
We can't help but wonder of the future that lies.
For a nation based on speed and scurry,
Frustration, ego, and constant fury,
Could it be we are rushing to
A new world to live in, a place
We all know as complete oblivion?

Flower of Beauty

Be my pretty flower,
Every day and every hour,
To grow to the skies above
With true and everlasting love.

When you reach the tip of a cloud,
Cry with laughter aloud
For you are a beauty and so real—
I need you to share all that I feel.

I am the flower next door,
Growing with you more and more,
And together we will stem
Into two happy gems.

I Need (a Job)

I need a gig, little or big, let me show my stuff.
I'll do even more and sweep any floor
'cause to pay the bills with no dough is rough.

I need some bread to get outta the red
and keep that roof overhead.
Without that work, I become a jerk
with a new home in jail instead.

Help is what I need,
a job will do indeed.
If I'm willing to give it a try,
don't let me go to waste and die.

I need to find just any old kind
of something I know I can do.
With these bare hands
I'll help till the lands
and keep them straight and true.

Simplicity

The purest crystal of life is to be completely ignorant of
the falseness in the world and to reflect the true, happy
sincerity of simplicity. *Simplicity in its greatest form* is not
simple.

The Feeling of Spring

The swishing of the trees,
Like the whispers of the grass,
Sing a song with the bees
That says, "We are here, alas."

The robins nod their heads,
The flowers begin to rise,
The grasshoppers flee their beds,
The birds take to the skies.

Oh, the beauty of the Spring
With its everlasting color
Will to each of us bring
The love that belongs to each other.

If they could only speak
And tell us of their lives,
I am sure that we would seek
To be as healthy, happy, and wise.

Creation of a Day

The songs of the birds fill the air with music.
The soft wind caresses the bright rays of sunshine.
The rhythm of the trees creates a tempo for the flowers,
and the green terrain makes a firm stage for this love
affair.
A sharp accent from the woodpecker is an obligato to
the cry of a peacock.
The sun finally rests its mighty head after a day of
brightness and gives way to the moon and the intrigue of
darkness.
Day becomes night.
The creation is made.
There is nothing undone.
The play has been fulfilled.

Dear, Sweet Mama

As I look into your eyes, I see the joy, pain, and sorrow of ninety years.

The love the children shared with you with each demanding day. Your beauty and brilliance have faded to the wraith of time and silence.

Do you look with passion or fear of a crumbling sphere? Are you content or just tired of the human behavior? Sometimes, peace and complete quietness are great remedies to restore our souls, but I'm afraid time has won its bid to take from you *the joy of living*.

~~~~~~~~~~

Mother's Day

Each day is Mother's Day for you, dear Javile. You've been a strong, basic honest hunk of raw earth to your children. You've given to all within your reach, and for those you couldn't reach, you gave more. You are an innovator, a pioneer, an original that shines through the darkest clouds. You will never know your capacity, but you will always know that the power that is greater than all of us has touched you with a great sense of responsibility.

You are a light, even when out, that radiates a hope to all that meet your eyes. With all your magic onstage, you will never be able to know and control the acts of passion and love to everyone. Your reward at the end of each day is to pray for those who have made you lonely. Your Love and Peace are within you. We will all have to try to match yours.

Bitter Sweet

How can the direction be turned from the cynical, and with an utterance to the meadow and beauty. Do the tears for loved ones dry on the faces of others? Why think of others in the same tone? Do we love, then love a different way? Do we test? How magnificent and how strong the cadence of happiness rings true. But this truth bends like a stick in the wind. Must there be the other thought?

First there is strength, and love, and kindness. As the colors take hold, one is too bright. The fascination of this light is to shade it and caress it to blend amidst. When it is tame, the other colors join to a lovely hue.

What propels such dimension? A whim? A whisper? An embellishment? The finale? Never really ending, but always pending—the sound of the Bitter, the sound of the Sweet.

Tribute to Milt "The Judge" Hinton

During the day, Milt, the wonderful judge, roams mother earth spreading his love vibrations to all.

At night, his star shines high above as a guiding light of peace. We are blessed to be living during the lifetime of a great humanitarian, Milt Hinton.

Milt, may you continue your great time pulse and Bass-ic structure of Peace and Love forever.

Another Chance

The sky starts to lift its weary eye.
There is still no score from the night before.
The vanishing of fear makes the air crispy clear.
Maybe today there won't be a fight if we follow the
glowing light.

Do We Really Know?

The hillside sings with color—
The flowers have each other—
The wind challenges the sparrow—
The reindeer spurn the arrow—
The rabbit is quick—
But the frog does the trick—
The tree leaves rustle—
The squirrel seems to bustle—
The chipmunk has his chatter—
The valley knows its key—
Do we really know all that we see?

M.U.S.I.C.

The music I hear is mass unity sounding in concert—
To face the harsh sounds,
Play them with finesse,
And transfer their love
To a composition complete
With dancing hands and feet,
Waiting for you as the intro
And me as the finale.

Reverie

Whoever you are, can you not see—
That your every mold is a part of me.
You must hear my pleas sing out to you
For your thoughts are as mine, they ring so true.

Visually I paint your beautiful face,
And kiss it gently with all my grace.
It is then I wish to share your strife
And taste your breath to sweeten my life.

Whatever force it is that creates the rocks,
Or demands the keys to our yielding locks,
May the heavens above, to each of us race,
And guide us to our meeting place.

A Touch of Beauty

When I look to the sky on a calm, clear night, I feel its
greatness surround me. The cool breeze washes my
face, and the stars glitter their joy. The happiness of the
big round moon makes me smile—then I note that the
clouds are smiling, too, forming a picture of realism.
Such a sight and treat for the eyes of a human! Here is
the work of Nature herself. God's beauty and gift to add
softness and love to life.

Lonesome

Every thought of you
Makes me feel so true,
As I make my way
Through the long, long day;
Then my head seems to fill
With a wonderful thrill
To know that God above
Blessed me with you to love.

~~~~~~~~~~

Little One Lullaby

May the good Lord always watch you with the spirit of
His love;
May He bless you with His teachings up above;
So dream on, my little one, dream on, with all your dainty
charms—
We'll welcome you each day with open arms.

May you start each day with everlasting smiles and joyful
pranks;
May you learn the good old meaning of "Give Thanks."
We will shower you with kindness, understanding, and
good cheer,
Dream on, my little one, for we are here.

Miracle of Apple Valley
(Peaceful Love)

The sun gives me strength that I may shine on you
peacefully, with love.

~~~~~~~~~~

The Beauty of You

Your pretty eyes are aware—
Of my continuous stare—
As I watch your every motion—
And decide to take a notion—
Our thoughts are in rhymes—
For our eyes meet at times—
And with this I hasten—
With a tingling sensation—
I think of asking for your name—
Or talking freely to be game—
Then I long to have you in my arms—
And lure you with all my best charms—
One so luscious and with a beautiful air—
Needs to be complimented, for this gift is so rare—
With courage strong, I answer to your song—
After all—this twosome in a way—
Might make history someday!

A Portrait of Billy Strayhorn

Every century or so the world is blessed with a talent that excels in all fields. A human being capable of love and spreading this love wherever he goes. His contributions number many, but Billy Strayhorn will always be remembered for his beautiful soul. His concern and love for mankind are a great lesson for all of us. His beauty and music will live forever. He has left us for the future world, and if we are lucky, we will find him preaching love and spelling beautiful notes.

One Big Rug

Dear Lord, we pray—
Not to have things our way,
But merely want to express,
Our complete happiness;
If our love is a pattern of art woven together,
Then bless everyone with his share forever—
Weave all these souls to believe in one thing;
What all the love and happiness one big rug can bring.

Sudden Love

As I count the days we've been apart,
I feel a sadness in my heart.
The days gone by are empty of love,
And the precious moments are in the wind above.
Now I rejoice, for I know at last,
When I see you our love will make up for the past.
Suddenly, you. Suddenly, Love.

~~~~~~~~~

Every Day of the Year

If you can remember
The things you surrender
To me every day of the year,
If you kiss me daily
With arms 'round me gaily,
Do it every day of the year;
Just think of me
As your little honey bee—
And don't forget that I'm the one
You captured on the run,
If you love me this way
And I mean the whole day—
Then I'm yours every day of the year.

"I'LL SEE YOU AGAIN ONCE MORE"

BY LOUIE BELLSON

I FOUND MY PEACE
WITH THE WONDERFUL MEMORIES OF YOU,
THE STRENGTH OF CARING
"QUIETLY, I DO
QUIETLY, I TALK TO YOU",
I SEE THAT ROAD
IT WAS JUST YOU AND I AND THE SKY,
WE LEARNED TO CRY AND
LAUGH AWAY OUR TEARS,
WE LOVED ALL THOSE YEARS,
I KNOW YOU ARE ALWAYS IN MY DREAMS,
EVEN THOUGH WERE MILES APART IT SEEMS, AND WHEN
I HEAR {YOUR/THAT} VOICE
IT GOES DEEP IN THE HEART OF MY SOUL,
I KNOW THAT SOMEDAY
LIFE WILL TAKE ITS TOLL,
I'LL SEE YOU AGAIN,
LOVING YOU AGAIN ONCE MORE.

Dave Black, Francine Bellson & Louie Bellson

Pearl Bailey & Louie Bellson

ABOUT THE AUTHOR

Referred to by jazz critic Leonard Feather as "one of the most phenomenal drummers in history," Louie played and/or recorded with such greats as Duke Ellington, Tommy Dorsey, Harry James, Ella Fitzgerald, Sarah Vaughan, and on Norman Granz's *Jazz at the Philharmonic*. A prolific composer/arranger, his compositions and arrangements span a broad spectrum of music, from jazz to symphonic works. He pioneered the two bass drum setup and was one of the pioneer clinicians, giving himself selflessly to the music education community. He also authored a number of books on drums and percussion, many of which are still in print today.